Date: 4/20/22

J 398.2454 HAM
Hamilton, Sue L.,
The world's wildest
werewolves /

PALM BEACH COUNTY
LIBRARY SYSTEM
3650 SUMMIT BLVD.
WEST PALM BEACH, FL 33406

XTREME SCREAMS

THE WORLD'S WILDEST
Werewolves

A&D Xtreme
BOLD HI-LO NONFICTION

An imprint of Abdo Publishing
abdobooks.com

S.L. HAMILTON

TAKE IT TO THE XTREME!

GET READY FOR AN XTREME ADVENTURE! THE PAGES OF THIS BOOK WILL TAKE YOU INTO THE THRILLING WORLD OF THE WILDEST WEREWOLVES ON EARTH. WHEN YOU HAVE FINISHED READING THIS BOOK, TAKE THE XTREME CHALLENGE ON PAGE 45 ABOUT WHAT YOU'VE LEARNED!

ABDOBOOKS.COM

Published by Abdo Publishing, a division of ABDO, PO Box 398166, Minneapolis, Minnesota 55439. Copyright © 2022 by Abdo Consulting Group, Inc. International copyrights reserved in all countries. No part of this book may be reproduced in any form without written permission from the publisher. A&D Xtreme™ is a trademark and logo of Abdo Publishing.

Printed in the United States of America, North Mankato, MN.
032021
092021

 THIS BOOK CONTAINS RECYCLED MATERIALS

Editor: John Hamilton; Copy Editor: Bridget O'Brien

Graphic Design: Sue Hamilton

Cover Design: Laura Graphenteen

Cover Photo: Shutterstock

Interior Photos & Illustrations: Alamy-pgs 6-7, 12-13, 16-17 & 18-19; AP-pgs 4-5; Barcroft Media-pg 44; Getty-pgs 32-33; iStock-pgs 1 (werewolf), 10-11, 27, 29 (inset) & 34-35 (background); LatinAmericanStudies.org-pg 9; Mahlone Blaine-pg 8; NASA-pg 1 (Moon); Marvel Entertainment-pg 35; Paradox Interactive-pgs 42-43; Red Door Audiobooks-pg 34; Scholastic-pgs 36 & 37; Sega-pg 42 (inset); Shutterstock-pgs 14-15, 20-21, 24-25, 26, 28-29 & 30-31; Sony Pictures Animation-pg 41 (bottom); Summit Entertainment/Helen Peril-pg 37 (top inset); Universal Studios-pg 38-39, 40 & 41 (top).

LIBRARY OF CONGRESS CONTROL NUMBER: 2020948029

PUBLISHER'S CATALOGING-IN-PUBLICATION DATA

Names: Hamilton, S.L., author.

Title: The world's wildest werewolves / by S.L. Hamilton

Description: Minneapolis, Minnesota : Abdo Publishing, 2022 | Series: Xtreme screams | Includes online resources and index.

Identifiers: ISBN 9781532194900 (lib. bdg.) | ISBN 9781644946282 (pbk.) | ISBN 9781098215217 (ebook)

Subjects: LCSH: Werewolves--Juvenile literature. | Werewolves in motion pictures--Juvenile literature. | Werewolves on television--Juvenile literature. | Werewolves in literature--Juvenile literature. | Monsters--Juvenile literature.

Classification: DDC 398.2454--dc23

TABLE OF Contents

THE WORLD'S WILDEST WEREWOLVES 4
HISTORY 6
WEREWOLF SIGHTINGS 10
BECOMING A WEREWOLF 16
HOW TO STOP A WEREWOLF 24
REAL WOLVES 30
WEREWOLVES IN THE MEDIA 34
ARE WEREWOLVES REAL? 44
XTREME CHALLENGE 45
GLOSSARY 46
ONLINE RESOURCES 47
INDEX 48

CHAPTER 1
THE WORLD'S WILDEST
Werewolves

Legends say humans who change into wolves and then back to human form again are werewolves. They attack their prey with great strength. Their powerful claws and sharp teeth destroy with no mercy. They are fierce creatures of the night.

XTREME FACT

A werewolf is also called a lycanthrope. The name came from Greek mythology when the god Zeus turned the human King Lycaon into a wolf.

CHAPTER 2

History

The word werewolf means "man-wolf." It comes from England's **Anglo-Saxon** language. Many Europeans believed in werewolves a few hundred years ago. People stayed behind locked doors when howls filled the forests at night.

Other half-animal/half-man legends developed in places where there were few or no wolves. India had were-tigers. South America had were-jaguars. Some places had were-snakes, were-bears, and were-pigs.

A were-tiger climbs up toward his prey. Some believed that powerful sorcerers could turn themselves into were-tigers.

A statue of a Latin American shaman transforming into a were-jaguar.

CHAPTER 3
Werewolf Sightings

A werewolf **frenzy** began in Europe about 1100 AD. Stories spread of huge, terrifying wolves. Trials were held for hundreds of people accused of being werewolves. Some people went to jail, while others were killed.

XTREME FACT

Officials sometimes put real wolves on trial.

Gevaudan, France, had an unusually large number of animal attacks between 1764 and 1767. People said there was a beast that looked like a wolf but was as big as a cow. It was a killer.

XTREME FACT

The Beast of Gevaudan killed 6 men, 15 women, and 68 children.

Hunters searched for the Beast of Gevaudan. Many wolves were killed, but it wasn't until two very large wolves were destroyed that the attacks stopped. Was the Beast a wolf? A **serial killer**? Or a werewolf?

Marie-Jeanne Valet, a young woman tending cattle in eastern Gevaudan, fought off a great wolf in 1765. A statue stands to her bravery in France.

People believed in werewolves as late as the 1800s. Sweden and Russia were at war during that time. The wolf population in Sweden grew rapidly. Some **superstitious** Swedes believed that the Russians were changing people into wolves and sending them into Sweden.

CHAPTER 4
BECOMING A Werewolf

Many folktales tell of people becoming werewolves. The most common way is to be bitten, but not killed, by an existing werewolf. The next **full moon** brings on the frightening transformation.

XTREME FACT

Some people believed a gypsy's or witch's curse could turn an unlucky person into a werewolf.

If you were a child of a forbidden marriage in France, you might become a werewolf. If you were born on Christmas Eve in Italy, some thought you might turn into a wolf. A person who worked instead of attending church in eastern Europe risked growing fur and fangs. If you were born on the night of a **new moon**, you could spend each month howling at the **full moon**.

People thought wolf drool might turn a human into a werewolf.

Stories claimed that if one ate something a wolf drooled on might be the start of a wolfie life. Or eating the meat of a wolf might end a purely human life. Drinking water from a pond where a wolf drank or from water collected in a wolf's footprint could change a human to a werewolf.

According to some myths, a human could turn himself into a werewolf. A magic **ritual** and a plant called wolfsbane might do it. Or wearing a belt made from the pelt of a wolf or the skin of an executed criminal might turn someone into a vicious, wild animal.

XTREME FACT

Wolfsbane is very poisonous. Eating or even touching the plant with an open sore could cause vomiting, weakness, and numbness. It can even kill. Its poison was often used on arrows when hunting.

CHAPTER 5
HOW TO Stop a Werewolf

How does someone stop an unnaturally powerful werewolf? Long ago, people simply avoided going out on the night of a **full moon**. Locked doors seemed the best way to stop a werewolf attack.

The most common method to end the life of a werewolf was with silver. In ancient times, silver was thought to heal. In the **Middle Ages**, people associated silver with the gods of the Moon. Tales were told of stopping a wolf with a silver bullet. Of course, it also ended the human's life, too.

Many people thought throwing **holy water** on a werewolf could destroy the beast. Some believed love could cure a human **cursed** with werewolfism. Wolfsbane in a magic potion could cure, but also likely kill.

XTREME FACT

Carefully stabbing a werewolf so only three drops of blood came out might be a cure. However, doing that is quite difficult!

Wolfsbane was once used to poison troublesome wolves attacking farm animals. It's likely how the plant got its name.

CHAPTER 6
Real Wolves

In real life, wolves live in packs of 6-7 or up to 20 animals. They have their own territory and usually stay there. They hunt deer, moose, and elk, as well as smaller animals and **rodents**.

Wolves do howl at night, but not at the Moon. They are most likely talking with each other. They let other wolf packs know where their territory is. The group also howls to bond the pack.

XTREME FACT

A group of wolves (or werewolves) is called a pack or route.

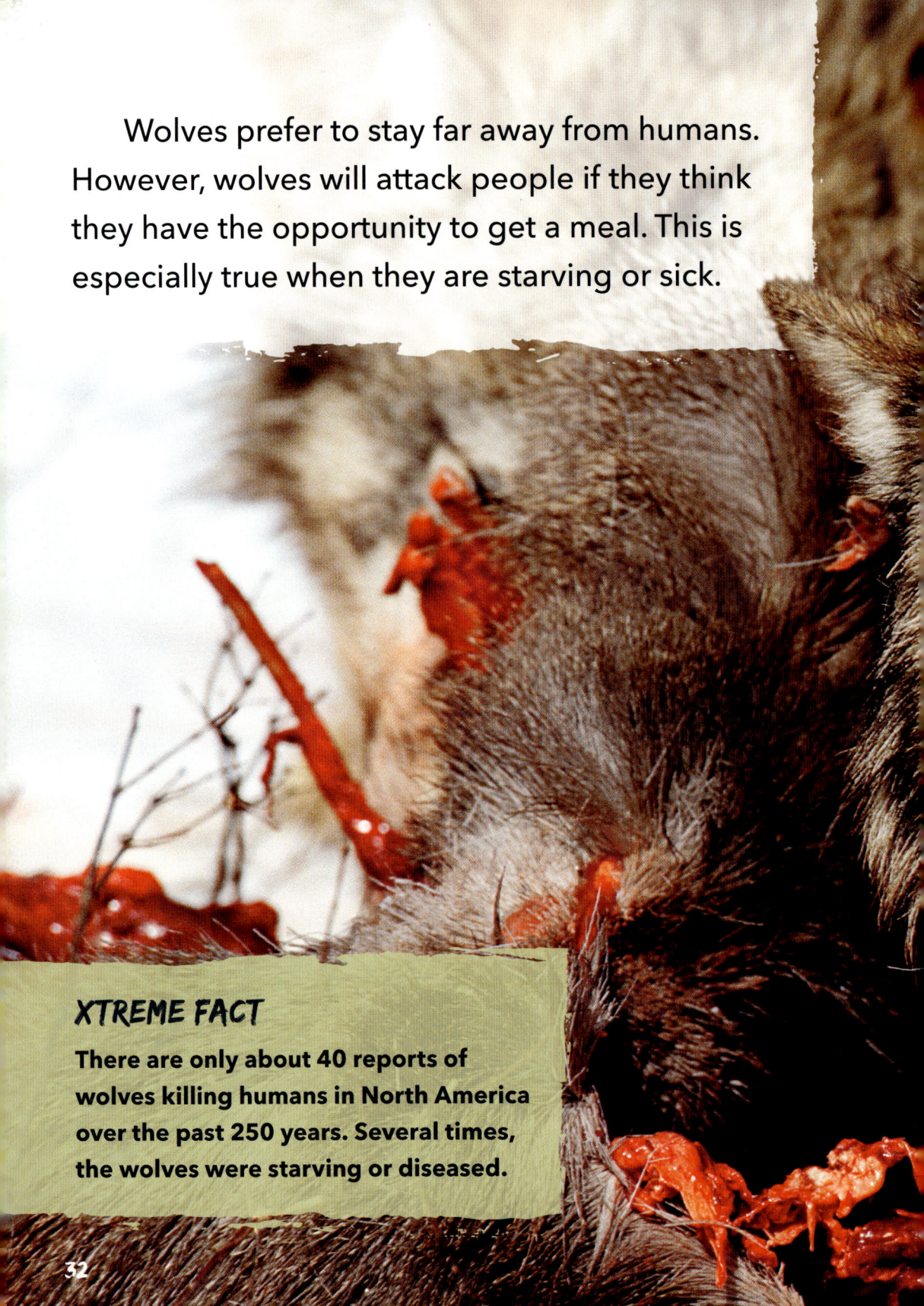

Wolves prefer to stay far away from humans. However, wolves will attack people if they think they have the opportunity to get a meal. This is especially true when they are starving or sick.

XTREME FACT

There are only about 40 reports of wolves killing humans in North America over the past 250 years. Several times, the wolves were starving or diseased.

CHAPTER 7
WEREWOLVES In the Media

Many books, movies, and games feature people who change into fearsome beasts and back to human form. *The Man-Wolf* was one of the first werewolf **fiction** books. It was written in 1831 by Leitch Ritchie. Hundreds of werewolf stories followed.

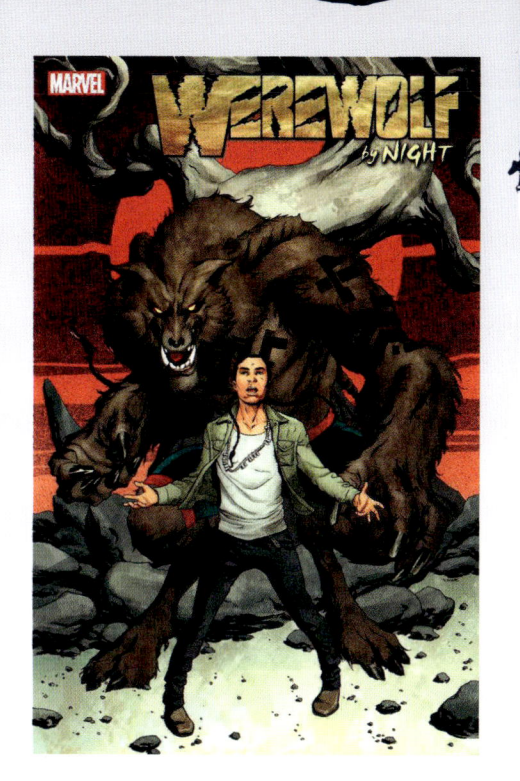

The frightening tales and fearsome look of werewolves make them popular in comic books, such as the *Werewolf by Night* series.

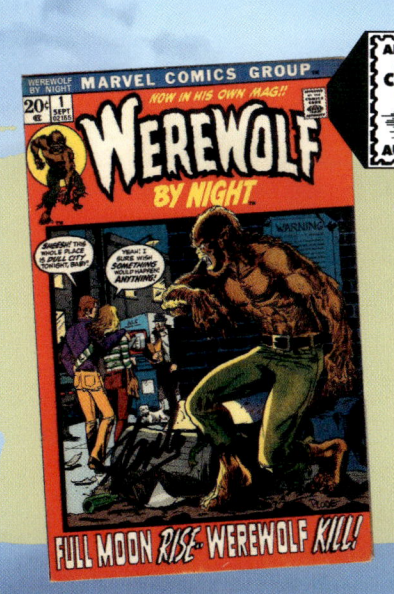

XTREME FACT

The Comics Code Authority was formed in 1954 to make comic books less terrifying. For many years, every comic book had to be approved by this group.

Millions of today's readers enjoy modern **fiction** books with werewolf characters. Some of the most popular werewolf characters have been created by R.L. Stine, J.K. Rowling, and Stephenie Meyer.

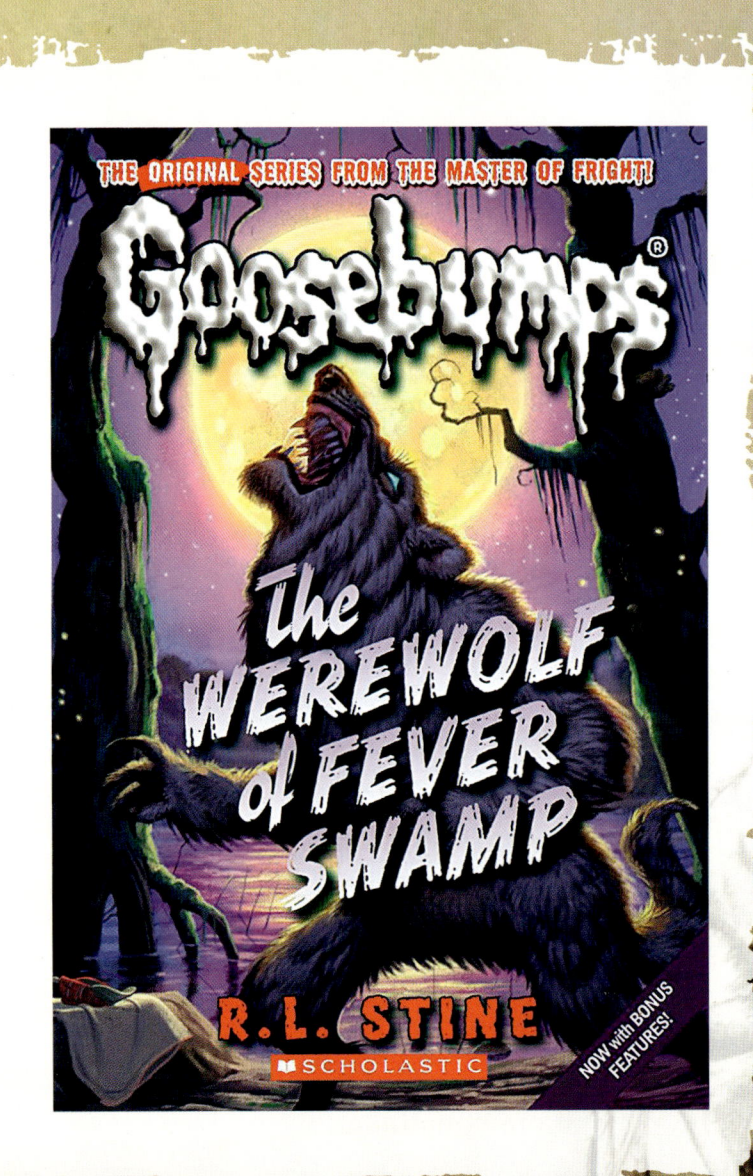

R.L. Stine wrote many werewolf fiction books in his Goosebumps series. His first was *The Werewolf of Fever Swamp*.

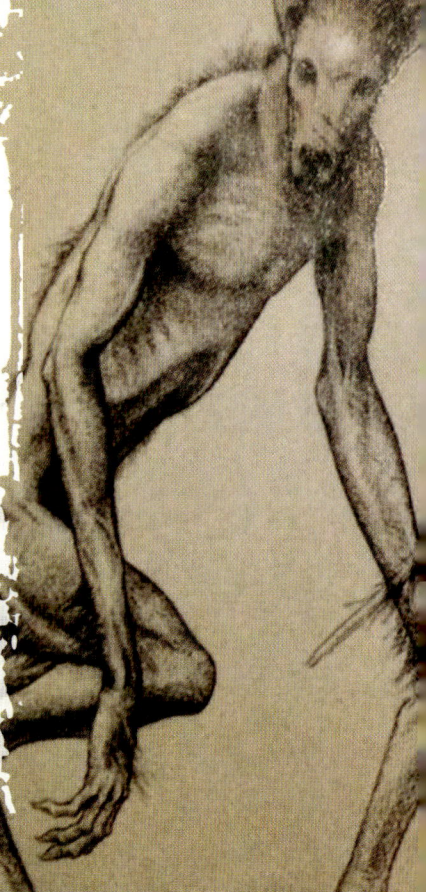

Stephenie Meyer's Twilight series, including *New Moon*, featured werewolves Jacob Black and other members of his Native American tribe. They transformed into werewolves at will and used their great strength to protect humans from vampires.

J.K. Rowling's Harry Potter series featured a teacher who becomes a werewolf at the full moon.

Werewolves have been featured in movies since *The Werewolf* of 1913. The most famous early werewolf movie was 1941's *The Wolf Man*. It starred Lon Chaney Jr. and became the classic tale of a man bitten by a werewolf who becomes one himself.

"Even a man who is pure in heart
And says his prayers by night
May become a wolf when the wolfsbane blooms
And the autumn Moon is bright."
— Maleva the Gypsy, *The Wolf Man*, 1941

XTREME FACT

Lon Chaney Jr. starred in five movies as the Wolf Man.

Benicio del Toro starred in the 2010 movie, *The Wolfman*.

Modern wolfman movies often feature the transformation of humans into beasts. Horror movies show the terrifying power of werewolves. Some dramas, comedies, and cartoons feature werewolves controlling their **lycanthropy** and living among regular people.

The transformation scene in *An American Werewolf in London*

Wayne Werewolf is a piano-playing, sheep-eating husband and dad in *Hotel Transylvania*.

41

Video games featuring werewolves often show transformations into vicious creatures. Gamers may play the werewolf or a human defending themselves against the fearsome creatures.

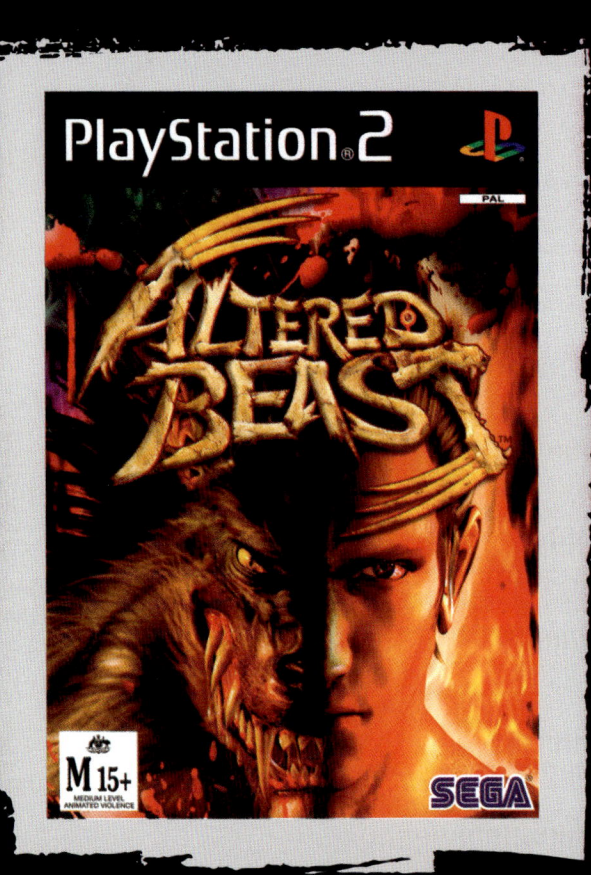

Altered Beast was one of the first human-to-werewolf video games.

WEREWOLF
THE APOCALYPSE
EARTHBLOOD

In *Werewolf: The Apocalypse Earthblood*, the main character of Cahal has human form for speaking, wolf form for exploring, and werewolf form for combat.

CHAPTER 8
Are Werewolves Real?

Hypertrichosis, or "werewolf syndrome," makes lots of hair grow on a human. The person may look wolflike, but it is just a rare medical condition. While some people believe in werewolves, most think the creatures are just legends designed to frighten and entertain us.

Hypertrichosis causes excess hair to grow on the face, arms, and legs.

XTREME Challenge

TAKE THE QUIZ BELOW AND PUT WHAT YOU'VE LEARNED TO THE TEST!

1) What is another name for a werewolf? What character in Greek mythology inspired the name?

2) What does the word "werewolf" mean?

3) According to legend, when does a human turn into a werewolf?

4) What poisonous flowering plant was thought to both cause werewolfism and sometimes cure it?

5) What metal is said to kill a werewolf? Why?

6) What are real wolves doing when they howl in the night?

7) What is the name of the medical condition that is known as "werewolf syndrome"?

Glossary

Anglo-Saxon – The Germanic/Scandinavian people who dominated England from the time of their arrival in the 5th century until the Norman Conquest of 1066.

curse – A series of words or a wish for something bad to happen to another person or thing.

fiction – Stories that are made up by a writer or speaker. Not fact.

frenzy – Wild, often crazy, activities that get out of hand.

full moon – A phase of the Moon when people on Earth see the entire Moon lit up. It looks very bright in a clear night sky.

holy water – Water blessed by a priest.

lycanthrope – Another word for werewolf.

Middle Ages – The period of European history from about the years 500 to 1500.

new moon – A phase of the Moon when people on Earth see only its dark side. It looks as if there is no Moon at all, or the barest outline of it shows. Also called a dark moon.

ritual – A ceremony that involves a special series of actions completed the same way each time.

rodents – Small animals with teeth that gnaw, including mice, rats, gerbils, hamsters, squirrels, and porcupines. Rodents are the largest group of mammals.

serial killer – A person who murders three or more people.

superstitious – A belief or practice resulting from a lack of knowledge or facts, fear of the unknown, or trust in magic or chance.

Online Resources

Booklinks NONFICTION NETWORK
FREE! ONLINE NONFICTION RESOURCES

To learn more about the world's wildest werewolves, please visit **abdobooklinks.com** or scan this QR code. These links are routinely monitored and updated to provide the most current information available.

Index

A
Altered Beast, 42
American Werewolf in London, An, 41
Anglo-Saxon, 6

B
Beast of Gevaudan, 12, 13
Black, Jacob, 37

C
Cahal, 43
Chaney, Lon Jr., 38, 39
Christmas Eve, 18
Comics Code Authority, 35

D
del Toro, Benicio, 40

E
England, 6
Europe, 6, 10, 18

F
France, 12, 13, 18
full moon, 16, 18, 24, 37

G
Gevaudan, France, 12
Goosebumps series, 36
Greek mythology, 5
gypsy, 17, 38

H
Harry Potter series, 37
Hotel Transylvania, 41
hypertrichosis, 44

I
India, 8
Italy, 18

L
Latin America, 9
Lycaon, King, 5

M
Maleva the Gypsy, 38
Man-Wolf, The, 34
Meyer, Stephenie, 36, 37
Middle Ages, 27
Moon, 27, 31, 38

N
Native American, 37
new moon, 18
New Moon (movie), 37
North America, 32

R
Ritchie, Leitch, 34
Rowling, J.K., 36, 37
Russia, 15

S
South America, 8
Stine, R.L., 36
Sweden, 15

T
Twilight series, 37

V
Valet, Marie-Jeanne, 13

W
Werewolf, The, 38
Werewolf, Wayne, 39
Werewolf by Night, 35
Werewolf of Fever Swamp, The, 36
werewolf syndrome, 44
Werewolf: The Apocalypse Earthblood, 43
Wolf Man (character), 39
Wolf Man, The (1941 movie), 38
Wolfman, The (2010 movie), 40

Z
Zeus, 5